Y O U R

F A I T H

P A T H

YOUR
FAITH
PATH

Discover How to Choose Your Beliefs

MARK MITTELBERG

WILLOW
Willow Creek Resources

Tyndale House Publishers, Inc.
Carol Stream, Illinois

Visit Tyndale's exciting Web site at www.tyndale.com

TYNDALE and Tyndale's quill logo are registered trademarks of Tyndale House Publishers, Inc.

Your Faith Path: Discover How to Choose Your Beliefs

Designed by Stephen Vosloo and Timothy R. Botts

Edited by Dave Lindstedt

Published in association with the literary agency of Alive Communications, Inc., 7680 Goddard Street, Suite 200, Colorado Springs, CO 80920.

Scripture quotations are taken from the *Holy Bible*, New Living Translation, copyright © 1996, 2004. Used by permission of Tyndale House Publishers, Inc., Carol Stream, Illinois 60188. All rights reserved.

ISBN-13: 978-1-4143-2045-8
ISBN-10: 1-4143-2045-0

Printed in the United States of America

14 13 12 11 10 09 08
 7   6   5   4   3   2   1

INTRODUCTION

You may not have realized this before, but *you live your life by faith*—every day and in many different ways.

So do I.

Let's think about it: We have breakfast in the morning—by faith—trusting that no one has laced our food with poison. We stop for coffee, trusting the barista not to put something harmful in our triple-shot, extra foam, grande lattes. We sit down in our chairs at work, without testing them first to make sure they'll still hold us. We key in private financial information on Web sites that claim to be secure, but we really don't know that they are. (We simply trust that the people who run the site will use the information properly.) We sign business and legal contracts, even though we haven't read the fine print—and might not understand it if we did. And we invest in the stock market. (If that doesn't take some faith, I don't know what does.)

There's no getting around it: You and I both live our lives by faith. We routinely make decisions and take actions that we trust will work out for our benefit—but we don't know for certain that they will.

We probably have reasons for most of what we decide to do, which is good, but we could be wrong about some of our conclusions. And some of those mistakes might be serious, even life threatening.

∞

What's true in the ordinary areas of life is also true in spiritual matters. Whether you're religious, into "spirituality" in some form, or skeptical about everything associated with the word *spirit*, you are *still* a person of faith.

You might believe in one God, many gods, or an all-encompassing god (of which everything and everyone is a part). Or you may believe there is no God at all. But regardless of your perspective, you base your beliefs on reasons that can't be known with complete certainty; therefore, you must make up the difference with trust, or faith.

Even the statement "There is no God" can't be proved, so it must be embraced by atheists as an article of faith—trusting that they have sufficient reasons to disbelieve in God and supposing they won't someday face a deity who will ask them to give an account of their beliefs and actions. That kind of trust is the skeptic's own version of nonreligious faith.

Because we all live by a measure of faith in regard to our spiritual beliefs, the important question is this: On what are we basing our beliefs? Put another way, by what means did you attain your faith? What criteria did you bank on and value? You've somehow arrived at your current point of view, but how did you get there?

From my observation, we come to our beliefs regarding God and matters of religion through a variety of approaches—what I refer to as *faith paths*. Knowing which faith path you're on is crucial, because the approach you take can have a huge bearing on which faith you end up choosing.

I realized this during college, when it became clear to me that I'd accepted my Christian faith without serious study, careful assessment of the information, or some deep spiritual experience or insight. Mostly, I'd just accepted what my parents had taught me. I had adopted a hand-me-down faith. That didn't make it wrong—but it didn't make it right, either. I had gotten my beliefs through the faith path of *tradition*, as many people do, but when my faith was challenged by a philosophy professor, I knew that I owed it to myself to pause long enough to reexamine my beliefs in light of logic and real evidence. I needed to make certain I was choosing my faith for myself (not just inheriting it somehow from my parents) and doing so wisely—based on reliable criteria.

Think about it. Don't you owe it to yourself not only to think about what your current beliefs are, but also to step back and consider *how* and *why* you selected them? Doing so can bring spiritual clarity, some possible course corrections, and, ultimately, real confidence.

The purpose of *Your Faith Path* is to help you identify how you approach faith decisions. Put more simply, my aim in this booklet is to help you discover which faith path you've taken to arrive at your current beliefs.

Once you've identified your particular faith path, I'll offer a few thoughts to help you evaluate how well that path is serving you, and whether you should consider additional or alternative routes toward discovering what's true and worth trusting.

I don't know where your journey will ultimately lead you, but let me assure you that it's an important one—one worth giving plenty of careful consideration. I'm glad that I reassessed the reasons behind my own faith when I was in college and made certain I was trusting in the right things. Personally, I don't think there is anything more important than thoughtfully and wisely choosing your faith.

Filling Out Your Faith Path Quiz

Here's how to take this simple quiz: Read the statements on the following pages and consider the degree to which each one describes you or your beliefs. After reading each statement, write the number that most closely reflects your response. Choose from 0 to 5, according to the following scale:

5 That's totally me.
4 That's usually like me.
3 That's often like me.
2 That's a little like me.
1 That's barely like me.
0 That's not me at all.

Don't spend a lot of time pondering the statements. Simply jot down your initial response, from 0 to 5, and move on to the next one. Repeat the process until you've written down responses to all forty-two statements.

_____ 1. What a person decides is true depends on his or her particular point of view.

_____ 2. I've never really thought about reasons for my faith; I just grew up believing it.

_____ 3. It would be unwise to question what I've been taught within my faith tradition.

_____ 4. Your senses can deceive you; you're better off listening to your heart.

_____ 5. I have confidence in what I believe because God showed me it's true.

_____ 6. Spiritual teachings need to add up logically; I don't have to fully understand them, but I can't believe anything that's self-contradictory.

_____ 7. You shouldn't try to tell someone else what he or she ought to believe.

_____ 8. My beliefs have been clear to me since I was taught them as a child.

_____ 9. It makes sense to give deference to those in authority who have the ability and discernment needed to evaluate spiritual matters.

_____ 10. I can just feel what is right or true.

_____ 11. It may have been through a dream, a vision, or an apparition, but one way or another I got "the message," and I follow it.

_____ 12. People have all kinds of hunches and instincts; if they're not careful, those can get them in a lot of trouble.

_____ 13. Whatever you believe is true for you.

_____ 14. I know by heart many of the words (of songs/ scriptures/readings/creeds) without necessarily knowing what they mean.

_____ 15. It would be presumptuous to second-guess the teachings I've received; I don't have the training, knowledge, or formal degrees.

_____ 16. My friends and I talk about spiritual things and decide what to believe.

_____ 17. I know my spiritual direction is right because I often sense God's presence.

_____ 18. I think we should just deal with the facts; it's okay if they challenge conventional thinking.

_____ 19. What matters most is that you are sincere in your beliefs.

_____ 20. I can hardly remember _not_ going with my family to worship.

_____ 21. If I don't follow what I am taught, I will suffer the consequences.

_____ 22. I know what the so-called spiritual experts try to tell us, but I have a hunch they're wrong.

_____ 23. You can study your books and consult the experts, but God told me what's right, and for me that settles it.

_____ 24. I'd like to believe things people tell me, but I've got to check it out first.

_____ 25. Tolerance means acknowledging that everyone's ideas are true and valuable for them.

_____ 26. I don't think I could ever believe anything other than my religion; our family has practiced it for generations.

_____ 27. I have a high degree of trust toward people whose talents, skills, and knowledge have brought them to positions of spiritual leadership.

_____ 28. I can usually tell within seconds if something is true.

_____ 29. When our group gets together to study or worship, we can literally feel God's presence, and that gives us confidence our beliefs are on the right track.

_____ 30. It's easy to glamorize "following your heart" or hanging on to ancient traditions, but the question is whether or not a claim is actually true.

_____ 31. It would be judgmental to say my way is right and yours is wrong.

_____ 32. I go to meetings at the church/mosque/temple/synagogue/group because that's our custom—it's just what we do.

_____ 33. Our book says it, and I believe it.

_____ 34. Generally, my mistakes have come when I've ignored my inner voice or my "gut feelings."

_____ 35. Whether it was an angel, a departed loved one, or some other kind of spiritual personage, I can't ignore the insights my experience gave me.

_____ 36. It's hard to argue with the evidence.

_____ 37. I can tell something is true by the fact that it's working in my life.

_____ 38. It's hard for me to think about *not* being involved in my particular faith; it's part of my whole heritage and identity.

_____ 39. It's a high value in my religion to humbly submit to what the leaders say.

_____ 40. I think many people have what might be called a "sixth sense" about what is right and true, and they need to follow it.

_____ 41. I didn't know what to think, so I prayed and asked for supernatural guidance, and I was given assurance about which way I should go.

_____ 42. I just try to weigh the information I'm given, carefully consider the source, and reach a logical conclusion.

Now copy the number you wrote by each of the statements to the corresponding blank on the chart below,

Relativistic	Traditional	Authoritarian
1. _____	2. _____	3. _____
7. _____	8. _____	9. _____
13. _____	14. _____	15. _____
19. _____	20. _____	21. _____
25. _____	26. _____	27. _____
31. _____	32. _____	33. _____
37. _____	38. _____	39. _____
TOTALS: _____	_____	_____
PAGES: 15–17	19–20	21–23

and total each column. This will help you to see which faith path you're currently on. Next, turn to the pages that correspond to your highest score (listed at the bottom of the chart), and consider the advice and encouragement you find there, addressed to your particular faith path. (If you discover that you're close or equal on two or three faith paths, that's okay. Just read each of the sections and consider the advice that best fits you.)

Intuitive	Mystical	Evidential
4. _____	5. _____	6. _____
10. _____	11. _____	12. _____
16. _____	17. _____	18. _____
22. _____	23. _____	24. _____
28. _____	29. _____	30. _____
34. _____	35. _____	36. _____
40. _____	41. _____	42. _____
_____	_____	_____
25–27	**29–31**	**33–35**

FOR THOSE ON THE *RELATIVISTIC* FAITH PATH

The *Relativistic* approach sees truth as personal, flowing out of an individual's experience, values, priorities, and perspective. It's not absolute, and it is not limited to any one person's or group's perception. Truth is measured by the degree to which it fits with one's other beliefs, and perhaps an assessment of how well it's working in one's life or in the society as a whole. This view of truth is rapidly becoming popular in our culture, especially in high schools and universities. It's not uncommon to hear it expressed with phrases such as "That's true for you" and "I have my truth and you have yours."

If this description fits your point of view, there's some good news and some *challenging* news. The good news is that you are probably a tolerant person—one who is able to listen in a nonjudgmental way to people of differing perspectives. This makes it easier to learn from the experiences and wisdom of others and to get along with people who see life—including matters of faith—differently than you do.

The challenging news? Though tolerance is a really good thing, and every person's right to believe as they wish should certainly be protected, saying that everyone's perspective is equally true is an impossible position to maintain.

You don't agree with that statement? That proves my point. The very act of disagreeing shows that you believe your position is right and mine is not. If you're really honest, you think that your relativistic position is more than just "your truth." You believe it's true for everybody. But that belief in itself undermines your multi-truth position.

The Relativistic approach treats truth as a by-product of the mind—something we invent rather than discover. But isn't it a fact that in every area of life we must find out what is true and then align our lives to that reality? For example, we don't invent the speed limit (though we may have tried)—we discover what it is and then abide by it or pay the penalty. If we're in school, we don't answer the questions on the test with what we want to be true or what fits our personal perspective—we do our best to give the correct answers, and then we're graded accordingly. And if we step out in front of a moving bus, it really doesn't matter how we view buses or what we believe about them. . . .

It's like the old saying: *reality bites.* It doesn't adjust itself to accommodate our sincerely held beliefs. Truth is simply what it is—with or without our points of view. So, we'd be wise to discover what the real truth is and arrange our lives accordingly.

If this discover-the-truth-and-act-accordingly approach governs the ordinary aspects of life, why should we suppose it is any different with spiritual things? The fact that something is unseen doesn't make it any less real. Poisonous gas is deadly whether we detect it or not. Whatever is true about the spiritual world is true whether we believe in it, like it, resist it, or ignore it altogether. If God exists, no consortium of atheists is going to vote him out of existence. And if he doesn't exist, not even the most fervent religious group will be able to pray and worship him into existence.

The important question we need to ask ourselves is this: How can we know what's really true in the spiritual realm so we can adjust our lives to that truth? To learn more about this, read the section in this booklet that addresses the *Evidential* faith path (page 33), as well as the general conclusion on page 37. Also, for a more in-depth discussion about relativism, truth, and the existence of God, see my book *Choosing Your Faith*.

FOR THOSE ON THE *TRADITIONAL* FAITH PATH

The *Traditional* approach is probably the most traveled of the six faith paths. That's because so many of us adopt our beliefs—as I did up until college—based on the religious practices (or lack thereof) we learned from our families. It's a natural thing. We grow up learning virtually everything we know from our parents and others in positions of influence in our lives—so why not trust them for information in the spiritual realm, as well?

In a sense, this method of "choosing our faith" is not a choice at all. It is more of a passive acceptance of something handed down to us. It's like an inherited custom or habit—which could explain why you sometimes feel as if you're just going through the motions of religion, carrying on traditions that may or may not have any real or deep meaning to you.

It's important to understand that finding your faith through the traditional teachings of your parents or family is not necessarily bad, and it doesn't necessarily make your beliefs incorrect. In fact, chances are that at least some elements of what you've been raised to believe are helpful and true. But traditions must be tested. They may be right, but they could be wrong. You'll never know until you examine the thinking and evidence behind the beliefs you've been taught, to see which ones are valid and worth holding onto.

Jesus, who at minimum was one of the greatest teachers who ever lived, would agree. He often challenged his listeners' uncritical commitment to hand-me-down beliefs, warning them that they were ignoring God's law and substituting their own tradition.[1] Clearly, he was not against *all* traditional beliefs, but he was strongly opposed to the blind acceptance of religious substitutes for the real truth of God.

One thing's for certain: Because different faith traditions often contradict each other, they can't *all* be correct. It's important, therefore, to stop and look at them more carefully.

Examining your faith traditions may feel inappropriate and even disrespectful at times, given family and cultural expectations that you'll just "carry on the traditions." But the hero of the story is never the one who simply goes along with the crowd or passively perpetuates the practices of yesteryear. Rather, the person we admire is the one who has the courage to see things anew, who bucks tradition if need be, and who embraces what's right and acts accordingly.

For help on how to test traditional truth claims, read the section in this booklet that addresses the *Evidential* faith path (page 33), as well as the general conclusion on page 37. Also, for a more in-depth discussion about tradition, truth, and evidence for God, see my book *Choosing Your Faith*.

FOR THOSE ON THE *AUTHORITARIAN* FAITH PATH

The *Authoritarian* faith path is similar to the Traditional faith path in that it's usually passively received. The difference between the two is that the Traditional approach is more about a *habit* that gets passed on from one generation to the next, whereas the Authoritarian approach is based on *submission* to a religious leader, teacher, or organization—past or present—and the ideas that the one in authority holds up as the standard to live by.

It's natural that you may have grown up under some sort of spiritual or religious authority, and when you were younger, you just accepted what you were taught without critically analyzing it. But part of reaching maturity in these matters is to come to the point where you step back and take a more careful look. It's important to really examine who and what it is that you're following to see if it really warrants your ongoing trust and loyalty.

Look at it this way: If you or your child becomes ill and you decide to visit a doctor, you're probably going to check out the doctor's credentials before submitting to his or her care. You're not going to go to just anyone who has the title of "Doctor." Doctors are not all created equal, so it makes sense to check out their credentials before trusting your health—or the health of a family member—to any particular medical "authority."

But what about your spiritual health—and that of your loved ones? Sometimes we apply caution in other areas of our lives, but we fail to scrutinize the authorities we trust in the realm of faith. Instead, we passively accept and pass on to others the beliefs that were impressed on us by an influential leader or organization in the past. Yet aren't good credentials equally important for the establishment of trustworthy spiritual authorities and teachings?

Jesus, a spiritual authority in his own right, repeatedly cautioned that misguided teachers would lead many people astray. He warned that false prophets would "come disguised as harmless sheep but are really vicious wolves."[2] The funny thing about wolves in sheep's clothing is *they look like sheep!* They dress and act in respectable ways, yet something is amiss.

If you're currently under a spiritual authority that does your choosing for you, let me encourage you to step back and think for yourself. You really do have a choice about whether you're going to allow that person or organization to keep leading you. But be careful about how you do this. Generally, there's no need to announce that you're reconsidering what you've been taught. Instead, quietly, humbly, and prayerfully begin to examine the evidence and logic that is supposed to support the beliefs you've been handed. Your research might end up confirming the validity of what you've been taught and actually reinforce the credentials of the leadership you're under. But it's also possible you'll find information that takes you to better conclusions and a wiser choice of faith.

Don't settle for simple answers or cave in to authoritarian pressures to just conform. Jesus said, "Keep on asking, and you will receive what you ask for. Keep on seeking, and you will find. Keep on knocking, and the door will be opened to you."[3] He also made a promise to those who would seek consistently and earnestly follow what they learn: "You will know the truth, and the truth will set you free."[4]

For further information on how to test the credentials of spiritual authorities, read the section in this booklet that addresses the *Evidential* faith path (page 33), as well as the general conclusion on page 37. Also, for a more in-depth discussion of the Authoritarian faith path, as well as evidence for God, see my book *Choosing Your Faith*.

FOR THOSE ON THE *INTUITIVE* FAITH PATH

People who take the *Intuitive* faith path tend not to trust in their intellect or what their eyes and ears tell them, but rather in an inner sense—a spiritual instinct that they believe points them toward right ideas and actions. Many examples could be given of people being guided or helped through this sort of spiritual "street smarts," or specific hunches about who to trust or what to do. If it's true that we were made by a wise and intelligent designer, it should not shock us that we might have some inherent ways of perceiving things that go beyond our five primary senses. That certainly seems to be true with the moral guidance that our inbred conscience often brings us.

The problem with trusting our intuition is that examples can also be given on the opposite side of the coin, where people have followed their instincts and hunches in dangerous and even destructive directions. These examples are usually forgotten more quickly and discussed less frequently than the positive ones, leaving us with the impression that our intuition is stronger and more reliable than it might actually be. It's interesting that King Solomon, the man considered by many to be the wisest who ever lived, warned, "There is a path before each person that seems right, but it ends in death."[5]

Our intuitive sense should probably best be viewed as an internal warning light indicating that further investigation is needed. But let me caution you not to use intuition alone, apart from more objective criteria, as the basis for choosing your faith. Think of a warning light in a busy intersection. The flashing yellow bulb doesn't tell you anything clearly or conclusively. It merely says, "Driver beware." It prompts you to look into matters more deeply by slowing down, heightening your awareness, and scanning the road left and right, as you search for more information and data that will help you know how to proceed.

That's a pretty good description of the Intuitive approach when it's working right. It alerts us to danger and prompts us to do whatever is necessary to further increase our understanding and inform our intuition. In other words, it tells us to investigate more deeply, and to check into other criteria to confirm what's true and to clarify the warnings we've sensed.

So, heed the "yellow light" of your intuition and look into the reasons behind what you are perceiving. Examine the supporting evidence, especially for whatever you might end up choosing to believe. Let your "gut feelings" confirm what you find, but don't let them lead you into blindly guessing or stumbling around in the dark, hoping to be lucky enough to trip over truth. Rather, turn on the brighter lights of reason and evidence by pursuing and considering additional, clearer information.

For further details on how to test your intuitive instincts, read the section in this booklet that addresses the *Evidential* faith path (page 33), as well as the general conclusion on page 37. Also, for a more in-depth discussion about the Intuitive faith path, how to discern what is true, and the evidence for God, see my book *Choosing Your Faith*.

FOR THOSE ON THE *MYSTICAL* FAITH PATH

The *Mystical* faith path, in which people believe they gain spiritual understanding through direct communication from God or his messengers, is an interesting one to assess. It is potentially powerful and important because if God really is divine, he certainly would be able to use immediate and perhaps unusual means to convey his message. But the Mystical approach can also be misleading if we mistake mere feelings for spiritual realities or wrongly identify real but dangerous spiritual entities as being good ones that are from God, which they may not be.

Consider these two equations:

FEEL ≠ REAL and **REAL ≠ GOOD**

FEEL ≠ REAL means that you can feel things that do not represent actual reality, including spiritual feelings that, although sincerely experienced, do not truly reflect God or his will. History and the daily news are filled with examples of people who thought they had heard from God but said and taught things that were clearly misguided. So be careful not to assume that real feelings always represent genuine spiritual realities.

REAL ≠ GOOD tells us that even if what we felt was real, it doesn't mean it was necessarily good or from God.

Jesus repeatedly warned against teachers who would do miraculous signs and wonders but were actually false prophets and enemies of God. Similarly, the apostle Paul, who had to scrutinize his own mystical experiences at various points along his journey, concurred with this caution. He acknowledged the fact that God can speak through supernatural means, but he also advised us to "test everything that is said. Hold on to what is good."[6]

In evaluating the Mystical faith path, we need discernment and the willingness to stop and examine what we've experienced—or think we have experienced. The popular slogan "question everything" is not far off the mark. The importance of testing things flows from common sense as well as from biblical instruction. It involves comparing what we've experienced to what we already know to be true—from facts about the world and from scriptures that have already passed the test of having reliable credentials of truth. It's from one of those proven scriptures—the Bible—that we are given this warning: "Dear friends, do not believe everyone who claims to speak by the Spirit. You must test them to see if the spirit they have comes from God. For there are many false prophets in the world."[7]

For more information on how to test mystical experiences, read the section in this booklet that addresses the *Evidential* faith path (page 33), as well as the general conclusion on page 37. Also, for a more in-depth discussion about the Mystical faith path, testing truth, and evidence for God, see my book *Choosing Your Faith*.

One final note: If you have a spiritual experience in which God somehow communicates his love or guidance to you—one that passes the tests and proves to be factually true and scripturally sound—then you have a great gift that can powerfully energize your life and faith.

FOR THOSE ON THE *EVIDENTIAL* FAITH PATH

This final approach, the *Evidential* faith path, is listed last for a reason. That's because it provides the criteria for testing—and ultimately supporting or undermining—the conclusions reached through all five of the other faith paths. Its two key elements, *logic* and *sensory experience*, are God-given tools that we must use to gain the vast majority of our information, to test truth claims and religious experiences, and ultimately to decide what to believe.

This may seem obvious (as you're reading this with your *eyes* and thinking about it with your *mind*), but we need to learn to intentionally utilize and apply both of these components. Real knowledge comes when the logical, organizing power of the mind is applied to the real-world experience and data gained through the five senses. These two elements are fundamental, undeniable realities. (To even try to argue against logic and sensory experience, we must first employ them.) And apart from them, nothing can be known.

When we apply these tools to the realm of faith, logic becomes a test by which we can eliminate self-contradictory spiritual claims. For example, any teacher who tells you that "all religions are really the same; they just use different names for God" fails the logic test. That's because if all religions are true, God is self-contradicting—and doesn't even know who he is! To one group, he's the omnipotent Creator who made the Universe but is separate from it; to another he (it?) consists of many gods, each worthy of some degree of honor and worship; to another he's the Pantheistic All who encompasses everything in the Universe in his infinite but impersonal divine Oneness (including you and me and our thoughts right now). Now, one (or none) of these viewpoints could be true—but not all of them! Sound logic doesn't leave open that option.

Let's look at the other component: *sensory experience.* This element wields *facts* and *evidence,* including information from history (the experiences of others, reliably recorded) and that which can be directly observed. Sensory experience can be used to investigate faith claims and show them to be false. (For example, when a faith claim is built on myths or based on mistaken teachings about the world, or when it endorses leaders who made prophecies that were purportedly from God but failed to materialize within their predicted time frames.) Evidence can also be used to build a positive case, as many teachers, writers, and speakers have done by showing the facts and evidence that back up the Bible and the Christian faith.

Now, I can imagine some people insisting that I've got it all wrong. They might say that God's revelation, or the scriptures, have to set the standard by which the other approaches are tested. I partially agree with this.

Writings that claim to be revelations from God, or scripture, once they themselves have "passed the test" and have proven to have the credentials for being trustworthy authorities, can and should then become a further test of other claims. But even then we must apply logic to make the comparisons.

The Evidential approach tells us logically and empirically that there is one set of truths—based on actual reality—that we need to discover and let inform our choice of faiths. We can use these tools to test the content of the multi-truth claims of relativism, traditional teachings, religious authorities, intuitive instincts, and mystical encounters, so we can know which of these are worth believing and holding onto.

We just need to stay open as we carefully (and prayerfully) follow the evidence wherever it leads. For more information on how to do this, as well as a discussion of numerous reasons why I think the evidence points powerfully to the truth of the Christian faith and the reliability of the Bible as a source of truth, see my book *Choosing Your Faith* (and the other resources recommended there), as well as the *Choosing Your Faith New Testament*.

CONCLUSION: CHOOSING YOUR FAITH

I love to go mountain biking. The trails I ride wind through the canyons in the foothills near our home. The scenery is stunning, with views of the higher mountains off in the distance and occasional glimpses of the Pacific Ocean out beyond the valleys. I often see deer and scare up a variety of other interesting animals. I love the aroma of sage and other fragrant bushes, flowers, and trees as I go blazing by them.

I should also mention that people sometimes get seriously injured while biking these trails. There are plenty of boulders, washouts, and cliffs that can send a rider unexpectedly airborne. Mechanical failure of the bike can also cause catastrophic crashes. And there are poisonous insects and reptiles, as a friend of mine will attest (he was bitten recently by a rattlesnake).

And then there are the mountain lions.

I thought the warnings were sort of a joke when I first moved to California—until I heard about a cyclist who was killed by a mountain lion about ten miles from where I ride. More recently, a lion was shot in the backyard of some people who live near me, and this summer another one was spotted at night, walking along our street!

I figured that because I ride fast I was probably safe. But I did a little research and learned that these cats—which can weigh up to 170 pounds and measure eight feet long from nose to tail—can run forty miles per hour and jump twenty feet straight into the air and up into a tree. And apparently, they are attracted to faster-moving prey, just like kittens are drawn to rolling balls of yarn.

Now I carry a knife and a cell phone whenever I ride (neither of which would probably help me, but California doesn't allow sawed-off shotguns) so at least I feel as if I've taken *some* precaution.

The bottom line is this: To at least some degree, *I ride by faith*. I don't *know* that I'm going to be safe or come home in one piece, but the evidence and the odds weigh in my favor. In fact, it's about as statistically unlikely to get killed by a mountain lion as it is to die of a shark attack—and the chances of either one happening are about 1/100 of the likelihood of being killed by lightning and 1/50,000 of the chance of dying in an automobile accident. So, if you ever go outside where you could possibly be struck by lightning—or, worse yet, if you're crazy enough to ever ride in a car—then *you live by faith much more than I do* when I'm riding my mountain bike.

That's just the way life is. We pursue our normal, daily activities with faith that they'll work out for the best—like they did yesterday. There's no proof or absolute assurance that this will actually be the case, but we work from the information we have and live our lives anyway.

Wise, spiritual faith—the kind I'm advocating—is similar. It is *belief* and *action* based on *good logic* and *evidence, trustworthy revelation,* and sometimes *substantiated intuition, credentialed authority,* and *tested tradition.* A reasonable faith moves in the same direction indicated by the facts, though it's a commitment or step that takes you further than the evidence alone can carry you.

Returning to my mountain biking example, I go out to ride when it seems safe, the weather looks good, and the trail is inviting. I think I'll come back home uninjured, but it still takes some faith (although only a little) to get on the bike. This faith is *action* based on *good evidence.*

Likewise, I believe in aviation. I accept what I understand about the science of flight. But just acknowledging those facts doesn't get me to Kansas City. I have to move beyond *agreeing* with the information and actually *exercise enough faith* (a moderate amount) to climb on board the airplane and fly to Missouri.

I honor the idea of marriage. But that belief alone didn't make me a husband. I still had to court the girl, pop the question, stand in front of the church, and say "I do." (That one took lots of faith—on *Heidi's* part!)

In each of these examples, faith entails two components: *right belief* (the bike is sound, the airplane will fly, the girl and I were made for each other) and *appropriate*

39

action (I'll ride that bike, fly in that airplane, marry that girl). But how do those components—right belief and appropriate action—apply to spiritual faith?

In my book *Choosing Your Faith,* I lay out twenty reasons for trusting in the God of Christianity. Many more arguments could be offered, but I'm confident that the ones I present there are solid and point toward truth—in other words, toward right belief. You can read about these reasons, which I refer to as *twenty arrows,* in the book—but here's a quick overview:

Arrow 1 ▶ Design in the universe points to an *Intelligent Designer.*

Arrow 2 ▶ Fine-tuning in the universe points to an intentional *Fine Tuner.*

Arrow 3 ▶ Information encoded into DNA points to a *Divine Encoder.*

Arrow 4 ▶ The beginning of the universe points to a *Divine Originator.*

Arrow 5 ▶ The sense of morality throughout the human race points to a *Moral Lawgiver.*

Arrow 6 ▶ The Bible shows itself to be a uniquely *consistent* religious book.

Arrow 7 ▶ The Bible is a uniquely *historical* religious book.

Arrow 8 ▶ The Bible is a uniquely *preserved* work of antiquity.

Arrow 9 ▶ Archaeology shows the Bible to be a powerful *verified* book.

rrow 10 ▶ The Bible shows itself to be a uniquely *honest* religious book.

rrow 11 ▶ *Miracles*, performed in the presence of believers and critics alike, point to the prophets, apostles, and Jesus as messengers of God.

rrow 12 ▶ *Fulfilled prophecies* point to the Bible as a divinely inspired book and to Jesus as the unique Messiah of God.

rrow 13 ▶ Jesus' *sinless life* backed up his claim to be the Son of God.

rrow 14 ▶ Jesus' *resurrection* powerfully established his credentials as the Son of God.

rrow 15 ▶ The *emergence of the church* points to the authenticity of its message.

rrow 16 ▶ The *changed lives of early skeptics* affirmed the truth of Jesus' resurrection and the teachings of the church.

rrow 17 ▶ The *willingness of the disciples to die* for claims they knew to be true affirms the trustworthiness of their claims.

rrow 18 ▶ The *changed minds of many modern skeptics* further support the Christian truth claims.

rrow 19 ▶ The *testimonies of countless believers* throughout history attest to the reality of God and the value of following Jesus.

rrow 20 ▶ It's true because *Jesus said so*—and he has the credentials to speak with authority.

ased on these kinds of beliefs, I chose years ago to ke appropriate action—by putting my faith in Jesus.

I understood the central message of the Bible—that I was a sinner (nobody in my family or circle of friends ever disputed that), that I deserved God's punishment (judgment and hell are unpopular subjects, especially when you realize you deserve them), but that God loved me enough to send Jesus to die on the cross to pay the penalty for my sins, in my place—and that all I needed to do was humbly acknowledge my sin and need and ask Jesus to be my forgiver and leader.

It's so simple, and it's based on truths that are backed up by so much logic and evidence, yet it seemed so hard to do. At least it did *before* I took that step; looking back I can't believe I even hesitated.

When I finally was ready to let go and follow Jesus, I simply prayed in my own ordinary and unedited words, asking him to forgive me and to take control of my life. It wasn't very dramatic, at least on the outside, but it changed everything. It was a step of faith that led to a life of adventure—and I've never wanted to turn back. I'm not claiming that life is perfect; just that it's better knowing God and living for him and his purposes, not to mention having the promise of heaven!

Looking back over the six faith paths discussed in this booklet, I'm glad I don't need to manufacture my own *relativistic* versions of wishful thinking, and then hope against hope they will turn out to be real. And it was after I quit clinging to *traditional* ideas that I ended up confirming most of the content and reasons behind the traditions I had been taught. Today, I can enjoy those traditions and pass on many of them to my kids—not as mindless habits or family obligations, but as proven practices that remind us of actual truth and reality.

I have an *authority* in my life that has not been imposed on me, but that I've willingly accepted and embraced because it—that is, *he*—has credentials like no other. And the revelation he has provided—the Bible—has established itself again and again as a trustworthy source of inspiration, spiritual information, and guidance.

Today, I actually have more reliance on my *intuitive* instincts than I had before, because I can sense that those instincts have been trained and tutored by God's wisdom. And they are actively balanced by the occasional quiet but real *mystical* leadings of the Holy Spirit. These come sometimes as simple impulses that draw my attention to a need, opportunity, or danger. At other times, they are more distinct impressions of God's presence or guidance.

And it's especially reassuring to know that my faith rests on solid *logic* and *evidence*. The use of these instruments for the testing and trying of truth has given me confidence that Christianity is not blind trust or a mere leap of faith. Rather, it is built on reliable data, history, and facts, as well as authentic experience. It's not just soothing and helpful; it's really *true*.

Knowing, following, and serving Jesus has been an incredibly exciting walk of faith—one I've never regretted and that I'm confident will never end. And it's from that perspective, as one not just convinced of truth but also experiencing an exhilarating relationship with our Creator, that I encourage you—no, *I strongly urge you*—to consider choosing your faith as I did.

> *"If you look for me wholeheartedly, you will find me.*
> *I will be found by you," says the Lord.*
>
> Jeremiah 29:13-1

NOTES

1. See Mark 7:8.

2. Matthew 7:15

3. Matthew 7:7

4. John 8:32

5. Proverbs 14:12

6. 1 Thessalonians 5:21

7. 1 John 4:1